Let's Draw!

Plants & Animals

Leon Baxter

Collins
in association with
Belitha Press

Let's draw together . . .

In the first six *Let's Draw!* books you discovered the basic principles
of line, colour, movement, shape and proportion. If you have tried
all those ideas, you should now be feeling more confident about
making pictures.

In these new books I am encouraging you to be observant and
inventive so that you will enjoy your drawing even more. You can
learn how to compose and construct your pictures, how to create
space and movement, and even how to have three-dimensional fun
with paper itself.

Don't use a ruler. Draw all straight lines freehand. This is a good
exercise for getting your eyes and hands to work together. Try out
some of these ideas. Use your imagination and see your paper come
to life.

Things you will need:

coloured pencils	paint	glue
crayons	sticky coloured paper	brushes
pastels	lots of drawing paper	scissors
felt-tip pens	(white and coloured)	

Have a good time!

Leon Baxter

First published 1989 by William Collins Sons and Co Ltd
in association with Belitha Press Limited,
31 Newington Green, London N16 9PU
Text and illustrations in this format copyright © Belitha Press 1989
Text and illustrations copyright © Leon Baxter 1989
Art Director: Treld Bicknell   Editor: Carol Watson
ISBN 0-00-197794-6
Typesetting by Chambers Wallace, London
Printed in Italy

Look carefully at these plants and insects.
Colour the picture.

Leaf and petal shapes

Here are some that I know.

There are lots of leaf and petal shapes.

You draw them here.

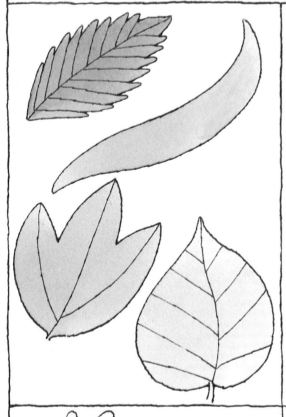

4

Often plants are small shapes that form together to make larger symmetrical shapes.

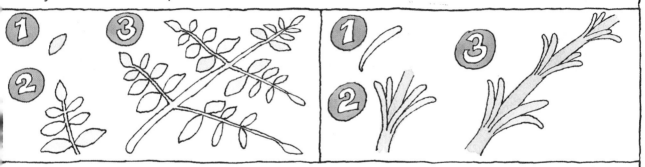

Sometimes little flowers grow closely together to form multi-flower heads.

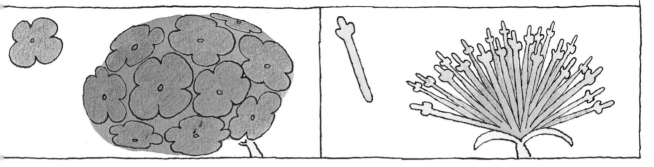

Draw some plants using single and multi-flower heads and different leaf shapes.

Plants like company

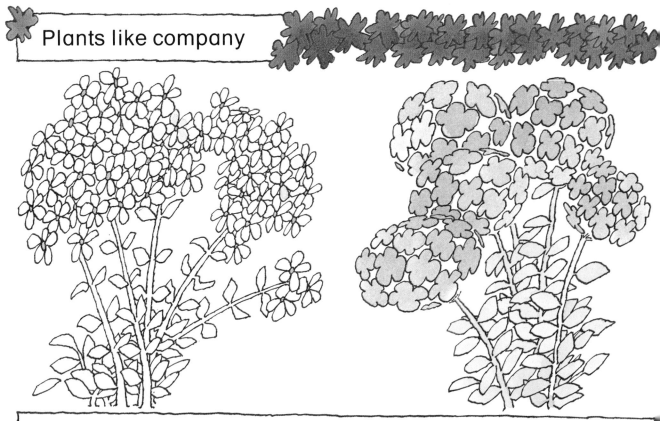

Draw groups of plants together. Think of the way they might lean and bend.

Silhouette trees

Trees are fun to draw even when they have lost all their leaves. Notice how the branches are thinner at the edge of the tree.

Finish this tree.

Trees are always changing. In winter the branches are bare; in spring fresh, pale green leaves appear; in summer the branches are heavy with leaves; and in autumn the leaves turn yellow and red. Can you finish this picture?

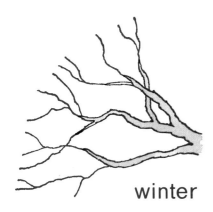

winter

autumn

spring

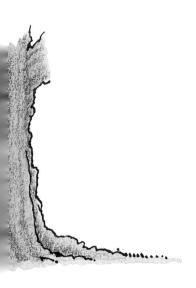

summer

Plants like the light. Their stems grow up and out.

Draw flowing shapes . . .

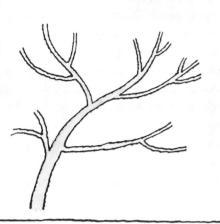

lots of leaves

put in the blossom

Use this space to draw a tall plant with leaves and a blossom.

10

Leaves can grow so thickly that they hide the stems.
You can suggest stems by placing the leaves and blossom
like this.

You try in this space.

Insects
Sur les plantes
If you look closely at plants you will find creepy crawlies.

Draw insects with three body sections.

Draw a big bug.

Draw insects with two body sections.

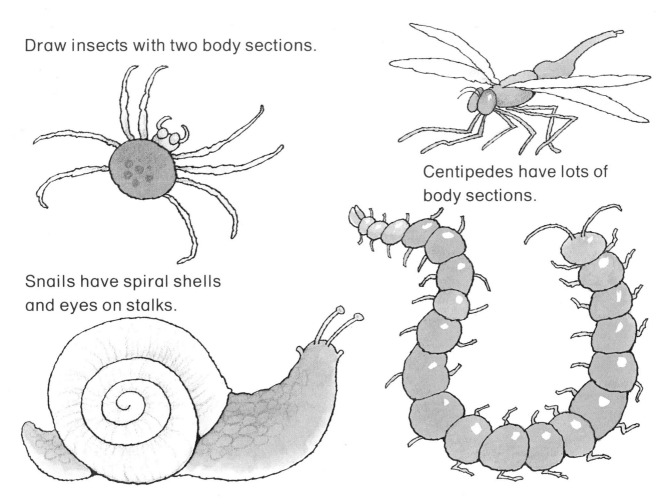

Centipedes have lots of body sections.

Snails have spiral shells and eyes on stalks.

Make a picture of all the creepy crawlies you can think of.

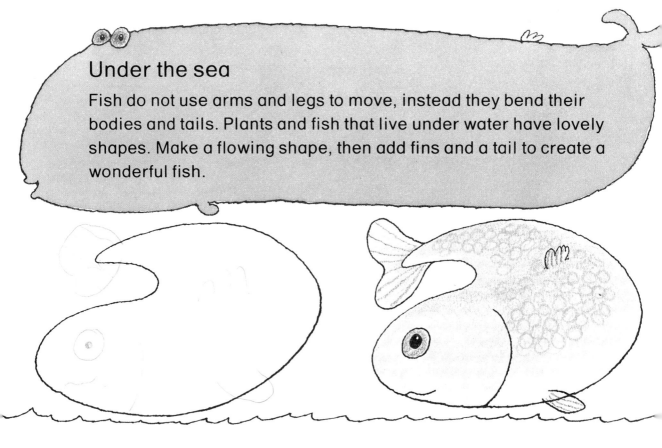

Under the sea

Fish do not use arms and legs to move, instead they bend their bodies and tails. Plants and fish that live under water have lovely shapes. Make a flowing shape, then add fins and a tail to create a wonderful fish.

Make a picture of the bottom of the sea.

14

15

Dog

I have used simple shapes to draw this dog and its puppies.

Can you draw a dog of your own?

Cat

Look at the shapes I have used to draw a cat and kittens.

Can you use the shapes to draw another cat?

Drawing a basic bird

Birds have skeletons similar to ours. This girl is standing as if she were a bird.

Birds have two fingers and a thumb within the structure of their wings.

Birds stand on their toes. Most birds have three forward toes and one back toe.

They have deep chests for the powerful muscles that move their wings.

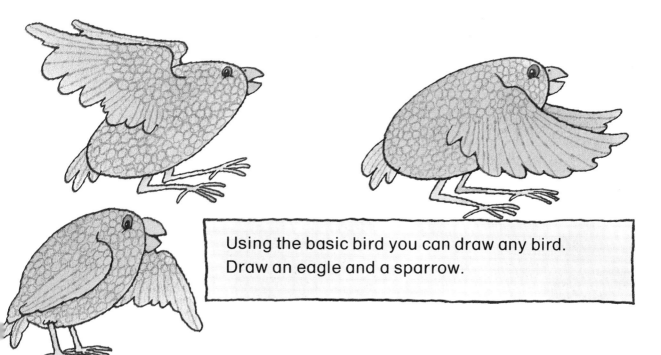

Using the basic bird you can draw any bird.
Draw an eagle and a sparrow.

Horses

Many animals stand on their toes. They have the same joints as we do but in different places.

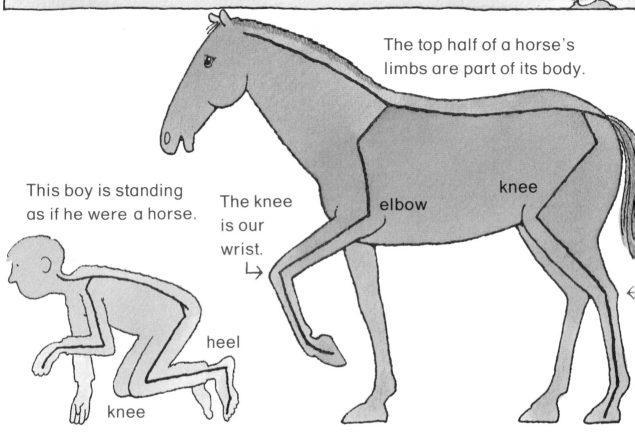

The top half of a horse's limbs are part of its body.

This boy is standing as if he were a horse.

The knee is our wrist. ↳

knee

heel

elbow

knee

The hock is our heel.

If a horse stood like you it would look like this.

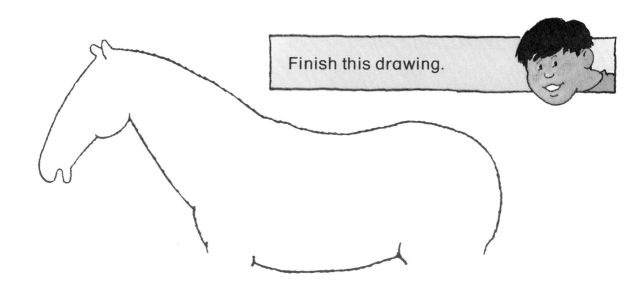

Finish this drawing.

Draw your own horse.

Antelope

Elephant

Lion

Rabbit

Hippo

Frogs

Can you draw the rest of these animals?

Birds

Rhinoceros

Wild boar

Crocodile

23

I have drawn some kittens and cubs.
Can you draw their mothers?